DATE DUE

	4	5	2

921
LOP

BC#32457105001634 $18.50

Gibson, Karen Bush
What it's... Jennifer Lopez
(bilingual)

Morrill ES
Chicago Public Schools
6011 S Rockwell St.
Chicago, IL 60629

LITTLE JAMIE BOOK

What It's Like to Be...
Qué se siente al ser...

JENNIFER LÓPEZ

**BY/POR
KAREN BUSH GIBSON**

**TRANSLATED BY/
TRADUCIDO POR
EIDA DE LA VEGA**

Mitchell Lane
PUBLISHERS

P.O. Box 196
Hockessin, Delaware 19707
Visit us on the web: www.mitchelllane.com
Comments? email us:
mitchelllane@mitchelllane.com

Mitchell Lane
PUBLISHERS

Printing   1   2   3   4   5   6   7   8   9

A LITTLE JAMIE BOOK

What It's Like to Be . . .	Qué se siente al ser . . .
America Ferrera	América Ferrera
George López	George López
Jennifer López	Jennifer López
The Jonas Brothers	Los Hermanos Jonas
Kaká	Kaká
Mark Sánchez	Mark Sánchez
Marta Vieira	Marta Vieira
Miley Cyrus	Miley Cyrus
Pelé	Pelé
President Barack Obama	El presidente Barack Obama
Ryan Howard	Ryan Howard
Shakira	Shakira
Sonia Sotomayor	Sonia Sotomayor
Vladimir Guerrero	Vladimir Guerrero

Library of Congress Cataloging-in-Publication Data:

Gibson, Karen Bush.
 What it's like to be Jennifer López / by Karen Bush Gibson; translated by Eida de la Vega = ¿Qué se siente al ser Jennifer López / por Karen Bush Gibson; traducido por Eida de la Vega.
   p. cm. — (A little Jamie book = Un libro "little Jamie")
English and Spanish.
Includes bibliographical references and index.
ISBN 978-1-58415-990-2 (library bound)
1. Lopez, Jennifer, 1970-—Juvenile literature. 2. Actors—United States—Biography—Juvenile literature. 3. Singers—United States—Biography—Juvenile literature. 4. Hispanic American actors—Biography—Juvenile literature. 5. Hispanic American singers—Biography—Juvenile literature. I. Vega, Eida de la. II. Title. III. Title: ¿Qué se siente al ser Jennifer López.
 PN2287.L634G53 2011
 791.43'028092—dc22
 [B]
                                                            2011014479

eBook ISBN: 9781612281377

What It's Like to Be... /
Qué se siente al ser...
JENNIFER
LÓPEZ

Jennifer López is an entertainer. She has been singing and dancing since she was five years old.

Jennifer López es una artista. Ha estado cantando y bailando desde los cinco años.

JENNIFER LYNN LÓPEZ

Dad
Papá

Sisters Leslie and Lynda with their mother and grandmother

Las hermanas Leslie y Lynda, con su madre y su abuela

6

Jennifer was born on July 24, 1969. She has two sisters, Leslie and Lynda. Although their parents, Guadalupe and David, are from Puerto Rico, the girls grew up in the Bronx in New York City. Jennifer ran track and played tennis at school.

Jennifer nació el 24 de julio de 1969. Tiene dos hermanas: Leslie y Lynda. Aunque sus padres, Guadalupe y David, son de Puerto Rico, las niñas se criaron en el Bronx, en la ciudad de Nueva York. En la escuela, Jennifer participaba en atletismo y jugaba tenis.

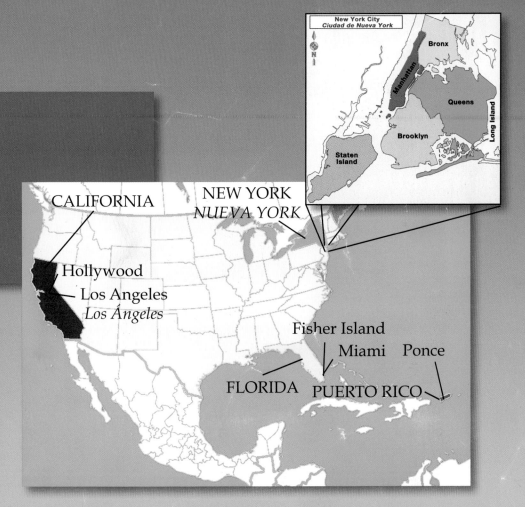

New York City
Ciudad de Nueva York

Bronx

Manhattan

Queens

Long Island

Brooklyn

Staten Island

CALIFORNIA

NEW YORK
NUEVA YORK

Hollywood

Los Angeles
Los Ángeles

Fisher Island

Miami

Ponce

FLORIDA

PUERTO RICO

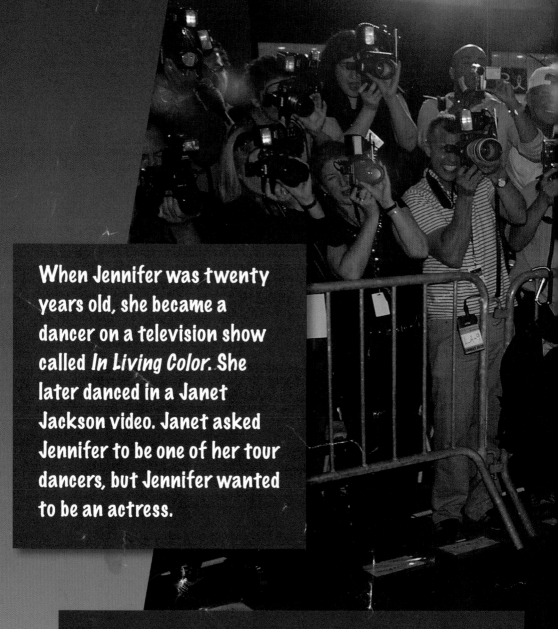

When Jennifer was twenty years old, she became a dancer on a television show called *In Living Color*. She later danced in a Janet Jackson video. Janet asked Jennifer to be one of her tour dancers, but Jennifer wanted to be an actress.

Cuando Jennifer tenía veinte años, participó como bailarina en un programa de televisión llamado In Living Color. Más adelante, bailó en un video de Janet Jackson. Janet le pidió a Jennifer que fuera una de sus bailarinas durante sus giras, pero Jennifer quería ser actriz.

The Fly Girls

Jennifer had acting jobs on television before she made her first major movie, *My Family*. Writer and director Gregory Nava liked her work. He asked her to be in another of his movies, called *Selena*. It was the true story of a Mexican-American singer who died when she was young. The movie was a success, and Jennifer became the highest-paid Latina actor in history.

Jennifer actuó en televisión antes de hacer su primera película importante, *My Family*. Al guionista y director Gregory Nava le gustó su trabajo. Le pidió que actuara en otra película suya llamada *Selena*. Era la historia real de una cantante méxicoamericana que murió muy joven. La película fue un éxito y Jennifer se convirtió en la actriz latina mejor pagada de la historia.

Selena
Quintanilla-Pérez

The movie *Selena* reminded Jennifer of something she missed: singing. She recorded an album called *On the 6*. She named it after New York's number 6 subway line, which she rode when she went to auditions.

Some people wondered why an actress was singing. To Jennifer, it was all part of being a performer. When she was young, her favorite entertainer was Rita Moreno, who sang, danced, and acted. Moreno won an Academy Award when she did all three in the movie *West Side Story*.

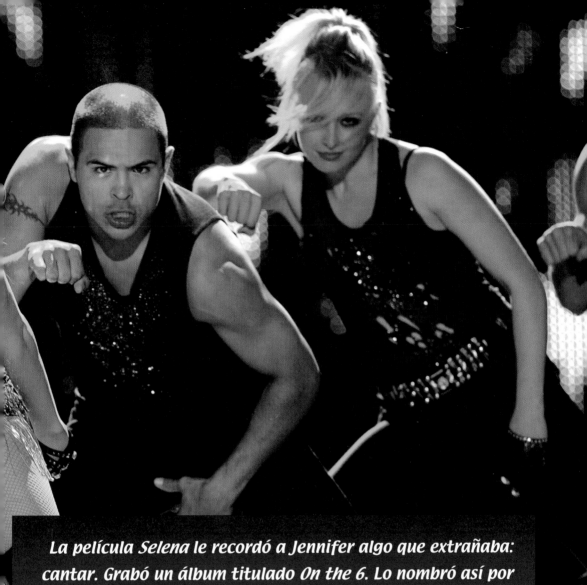

La película *Selena* le recordó a Jennifer algo que extrañaba: cantar. Grabó un álbum titulado *On the 6*. Lo nombró así por la línea de metro número 6 de Nueva York, en la que viajaba para ir a las audiciones.

Algunos se preguntaban qué hacía una actriz cantando. Para Jennifer, todo formaba parte de ser artista. Cuando joven, su artista favorita era Rita Moreno, que cantaba, bailaba y actuaba. Moreno ganó un premio de la Academia cuando hizo las tres cosas en *West Side Story*.

Jennifer in the movie
The Back-up Plan

Jennifer en la película
The Back-up Plan

14

Jennifer's second album, *J. Lo*, became the number one record. At the same time, her film *The Wedding Planner* was the number one movie. No one had ever had a number one album and number one movie at the same time before. J. Lo became one of Jennifer's nicknames. Another nickname is Jenny from the Block, taken from a song title.

El segundo álbum de Jennifer, J. Lo, alcanzó el número uno. Al mismo tiempo, su película The Wedding Planner subió al número uno. Nadie había tenido nunca un álbum y una película en el número uno, al mismo tiempo. J. Lo se convirtió en uno de los apodos de Jennifer. Otro es Jenny from the Block (Jenny, la del Barrio), tomado del título de una canción.

Her music album *J. Lo*

Su álbum musical J. Lo

Since then, Jennifer has released more successful albums and hit singles. In 2007, she released her first Spanish language album, *Como ama una mujer.* Marc Anthony, her husband, produced the album. Marc is also a singer. He and Jennifer sometimes perform together in songs and in movies.

Desde entonces, Jennifer ha producido más álbumes y singles exitosos. En el 2007, sacó su primer álbum en español, Como ama una mujer. Marc Anthony, su esposo, produjo el álbum. Marc también es cantante. Él y Jennifer a veces actúan, cantan y hacen películas juntos.

As a beautiful and talented star, Jennifer receives a lot of attention for her healthy looks. She stays in shape by exercising. In 2008, she ran, swam, and biked in a three-part race called a triathlon.

Como es una estrella bella y talentosa, Jennifer recibe mucha atención por su aspecto saludable. Se mantiene en forma haciendo ejercicio. En el 2008, corrió, nadó y montó bicicleta en una carrera llamada triatlón.

Jennifer has modeled for fashion designers and companies that sell beauty products. Glow is the first of many perfumes from her own company, Jennifer López Beauty. She has also produced clothing lines. In 2011, her clothing line for women was paired with Marc Anthony's line for men.

Jennifer ha modelado para diseñadores de moda y compañías que venden productos de belleza. Glow es el primero de los muchos perfumes de su propia empresa, Jennifer López Beauty. También ha producido líneas de ropa. En el 2011, su línea de ropa femenina salió al mercado junto con la línea de ropa masculina de Marc Anthony.

Jennifer and her JustSweet Collection

Jennifer y su colección JustSweet

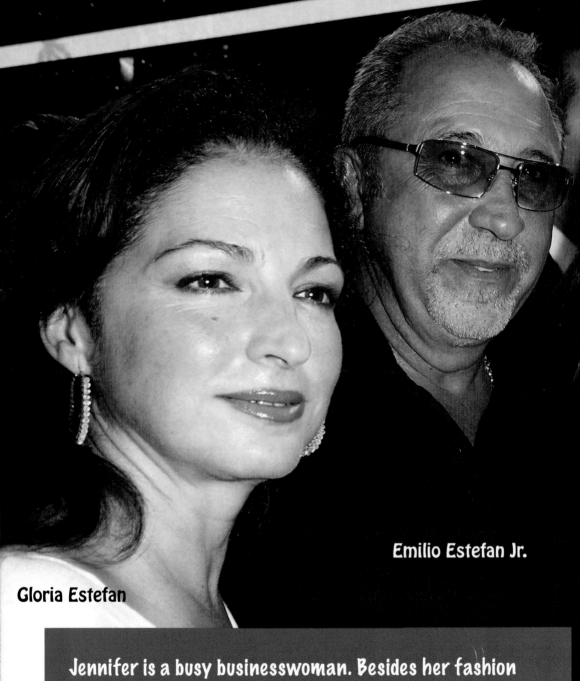

Emilio Estefan Jr.

Gloria Estefan

Jennifer is a busy businesswoman. Besides her fashion and beauty companies, she also owns a football team with her husband. They are part owners of the Miami Dolphins with Gloria Estefan and Emilio Estefan Jr., and sisters Venus and Serena Williams.

Marc Anthony

Jennifer es una empresaria con muchas cosas entre manos. Además de sus compañías de moda y belleza, también es dueña, junto con su esposo, de un equipo de fútbol americano. Comparten la propiedad de los Dolphins de Miami con Gloria y Emilio Estefan, y con las hermanas Venus y Serena Williams.

EMME

Jennifer and Marc have twin children, Emme and Max. When the twins were two, they joined their mother in an ad for the Gucci Children's Collection. Gucci gave one million dollars to UNICEF to celebrate. The company also gave $50,000 to one of Jennifer's charities called the Maribel Foundation.

Jennifer y Marc tienen gemelos, Emme y Max. Cuando los gemelos tenían dos años, aparecieron junto a su mamá en un anuncio para la colección de niños de Gucci. Gucci le dio un millón de dólares a la UNICEF para celebrarlo. La empresa también le dio $50,000 a una de las organizaciones de beneficencia de Jennifer, la Fundación Maribel.

Twins Emme and Max were born on February 22, 2008. Emme is one minute older than Max.

Los gemelos Emme y Max nacieron el 22 de febrero de 2008. Emme es un minuto mayor que Max.

Jennifer also helps other charities, including Children's Hospital Los Angeles. She became a spokesperson for the Boys and Girls Clubs of America (BGCA). Jennifer remembers belonging to BGCA when she was growing up in New York. A picture of her as an adult and one of her as a young girl are on a billboard for BGCA.

Jennifer también ayuda a otras beneficencias que incluyen el Hospital de Niños de Los Ángeles. También es vocera de Boys and Girls Clubs of America (BGCA). Jennifer recuerda que, de pequeña, perteneció a BGCA en Nueva York. Una foto de ella de adulta y otra de niña aparecen en los anuncios de BGCA.

Fans were excited when Jennifer agreed to be a judge on the popular television show *American Idol*. Jennifer likes new challenges. She leads an exciting life, and everywhere she goes, people want to know, "What's it like to be Jennifer López?"

A sus admiradores les encantó que Jennifer aceptara ser jueza en el popular programa de televisión American Idol. Jennifer adora tener nuevos retos. Lleva una vida emocionante y, en todas partes la gente le pregunta: "¿Qué se siente al ser Jennifer López?".

With fellow judges Steven
Tyler and Randy Jackson

*Con los jueces Steven Tyler
y Randy Jackson*

JENNIFER LÓPEZ ALBUMS
ÁLBUMES DE JENNIFER LÓPEZ

2011 *Love?*
2007 *Como ama una mujer*
       Brave
2005 *Rebirth*
2002 *This Is Me... Then*
       J to Tha L-O!: The Remixes
2001 *J. Lo*
1999 *On the 6*

JENNIFER LÓPEZ MOVIES
PELÍCULAS DE JENNIFER LÓPEZ

2010 *The Back-up Plan*
2006 *El Cantante*
       Bordertown
2005 *An Unfinished Life*
       Monster-in-Law
2004 *Shall We Dance*
       Jersey Girl
2003 *Gigli*
2002 *Maid in Manhattan*
       Enough
2001 *Angel Eyes*
       The Wedding Planner
2000 *The Cell*

1998 *Antz*
       Out of Sight
1997 *U Turn*
       Anaconda
       Selena
1996 *Blood and Wine*
       Jack
1995 *Money Train*
       My Family
1986 *My Little Girl*

FURTHER READING/LECTURAS RECOMENDADAS

On the Internet/En Internet

Jennifer López—Official Site
http://www.jenniferlopez.com/

Jennifer López Beauty
http://www.jenniferlopezbeauty.
com/templates/

Works Consulted/Obras consultadas

Boys and Girls Clubs of America:
Denzel Washington Announces
Jennifer López Will Join Him As
National Spokesperson For BGCA,
November 29, 2010. http://www.
bgca.org/newsevents/TheScoop/
Pages/JLoSpokesperson112910.aspx

Friedman, Roger. "JLo Has Billion
Dollar Backer for Do-Little Charity."
Showbiz 411, October 25, 2010,
http://www.showbiz411.
com/2010/10/25/jlo-has-billion-
dollar-backer-for-do-little-charity

IMDB: Jennifer López. http://www.
imdb.com/name/nm0000182/

"Jennifer López: Barbara Walters' 10
Most Fascinating People of 2010."
http://www.youtube.com/
watch?v=x1tcn0uAUSc

The Maribel Foundation
http://www.jenniferLópez-
foundation.org/

Nagel, Andrea. "L'Oréal Names López
for EverSleek." *Women's Wear Daily*,
December 3, 2010, Vol. 200 Issue 116,
p. 10.

Watson, Chris. "Jennifer López,
2001–2010." *The Newcastle
[Australia] Herald*, October 22, 2010.

Weinman, Jaime J. "Judge Jennifer."
Macleans, October 4, 2010, Vol. 123
Issue 38, pp. 80–82.

INDEX/ÍNDICE

American Idol 28–29

Anthony, Marc (husband / esposo) 17, 21, 22–23, 25

Back-up Plan, The 14

Boys and Girls Clubs of America 26–27

Como ama una mujer 17

Estefan, Gloria and Emilio / Estefan, Gloria y Emilio 22–23

Fly Girls, The 9

Glow 21

Gucci 25

In Living Color 8

Jackson, Janet 8

Jackson, Randy 29

J. Lo (album / álbum) 15

JustSweet Collection / Colección JustSweet 21

López, Jennifer
  as an actress / como actriz 8, 10, 12–13, 15
  birth / nacimiento 7
  charity / beneficencia 25, 26–27
  childhood / infancia 4, 7, 26–27

children (Max and Emme) / hijos (Max y Emme) 24–25

as a dancer / como bailarina 4, 8

family / familia 6, 7, 24, 25

as fashion designer / como diseñadora de modas 21, 22–23

hobbies / pasatiempos 7, 19

nicknames / apodos 15

as a singer / como cantante 4, 12–13, 15, 17

Miami Dolphins / Dolphins de Miami 22–23

Moreno, Rita 12–13

My Family 10

Nava, Gregory 10

On the 6 12–13

Quintanilla-Pérez, Selena 10

Selena 10, 12–13

Tyler, Steven 28, 29

Wedding Planner, The 15

Williams, Venus and Serena / Williams, Venus y Serena 22–23

ABOUT THE AUTHOR: Karen Bush Gibson has written more than 30 educational books about famous people, different cultures, and historical events. She has written about Barack Obama, Adrian Peterson, and George López. She lives with her family in Oklahoma.

ACERCA DE LA AUTORA: Karen Bush Gibson ha escrito más de 30 libros educacionales sobre gente famosa, culturas diferentes y acontecimientos históricos. Ha escrito sobre Barack Obama, Adrian Peterson y George López. Vive con su familia en Oklahoma.

ABOUT THE TRANSLATOR: Eida de la Vega was born in Havana, Cuba, and now lives in New Jersey with her mother, her husband, and her two children. Eida has worked at Lectorum/Scholastic, and as editor of the magazine *Selecciones del Reader's Digest*.

ACERCA DE LA TRADUCTORA: Eida de la Vega nació en La Habana, Cuba, y ahora vive en Nueva Jersey con su madre, su esposo y sus dos hijos. Ha trabajado en Lectorum/Scholastic y, como editora, en la revista *Selecciones del Reader's Digest*.